BIG BOOK OF RESCUE VEHICLES

Caroline Bingham

DORLING KINDERSLEY PUBLISHING, INC.
www.dk.com

A DORLING KINDERSLEY BOOK
www.dk.com

Project Editor Caroline Bingham
Art Editor Mandy Earey

Senior Managing Editor Sarah Phillips
Deputy Art Director Mark Richards
DTP Designer Megan Clayton
Production Josie Alabaster
Photography Richard Leeney
Jacket Design Piers Tilbury

First published in Great Britain in 2000
by Dorling Kindersley Limited,
9 Henrietta Street, London WC2E 8PS

First American edition, 2000
Published in the United States by Dorling Kindersley Publishing, Inc.
95 Madison Avenue, New York, New York 10016

Library of Congress Cataloguing-in-Publication Data

Bingham, Caroline, 1962-
DK big book of rescue vehicles / by Caroline Bingham.–1st American ed.
p.cm.
Summary: Text and detailed photographs explain how various emergency vehicles work, including the fire engine, rescue hovercraft, and snowmobile and rescue sled.
ISBN 0-7894-5454-8
1. Emergency vehicles–Juvenile literature. 2. Rescue work–Juvenile literature. [1. Emergency vehicles. 2. Rescue work.] I. Title.

TL235.8.B56 2000
629.04 21–dc21 99-042517

Color reproduction by Classicscan, Singapore
Printed and bound in Spain by Artes Graficas Toledo
D.L. TO: 35-2000

Dorling Kindersley would like to thank: Kelly Andersson; Steve Hinch and Melissa Renfrow at Aberdeen Fire Department, Maryland; Bryan MacCormack at Bombardier Aerospace, Canada; the Cockermouth Mountain Rescue Team; Dennis Hubbard at Erickson Air-Crane Co., Oregon; Phillip Orlandella, Gregory Mooney, and the fire crew at Logan Airport, East Boston, Massachusetts; Steve Maslansky; Captain Gavin Mills at NSW Fire Brigades, Australia; Flt Lt Phil Merritt and Flt Lt Greg Kelly at RAF Boulmer, England; the RNLI crew at Weymouth, England; John MacGraph, David Percy, and the crew of the Search and Rescue Hovercraft, Richmond, British Columbia; William Zander and the crew of the fireboat at Seattle Fire Department; Brent Friedman and David Chadwick at the Volunteer Medical Service Corps of Lansdale, Pennsylvania.

The publisher would like to thank the following for their kind permission to reproduce their photographs:
c=center, t=top, b=bottom, l=left, r=right

Bill Baker Vehicles Ltd: 28tl; **Bombardier Aerospace:** 3cl, 16-18, 19tr; **Colorific:** 12cl; **Crown Copyright Sect:** 23tr; **George Hall:** 11tr; **Tom Story:** 3clb, 19c, 19b, 20tl, 20-21, 21tr.

VOL. MEDICAL
SERVICE CORPS
345-7
MOUNTAIN RESCUE
COCKERMOUTH MOUNTAIN RESCUE TEAM
G693 NHH
N189AC
46
RAF
RESCUE
52-46
Lifeboats
RNLI
Canada
Coast Guard
Garde côtière
FIRE
RESCUE
CHIEF SEATTLE

Fire engine

Everybody recognizes the wail of a fire engine's siren. It warns drivers to move out of the way because the fire engine is in a hurry. There may be a fire, or somebody may be stuck in a tree. This fire engine has a platform on the end of a ladder. It is used to lift firefighters high into the air.

Going up – or down!
An aerial platform telescopes out and up on the end of a long boom. This one can be raised 102 feet (31 meters): as high as a 7-story building. The ladder can also rotate 360 degrees. It can even drop down to allow people to step off at ground level.

Outriggers provide stability

Fixed floodlight

This bag can be carried into an apartment. It contains small hoses

This panel controls the air supply from the oxygen bottle to the platform

Oxygen bottle

The boom rests on a plate that can turn a complete circle

Fold down step for access to boom

Exhaust pipe

Water intake valve

Water discharge valve

Two crew members can sit in here

One of the fire engine's lockers.

Throw in a mop

The fire engine has plenty of lockers, each packed with useful equipment. Extension ladders, traffic cones, shovels, pitchforks, and a chain saw are among the things carried. There is even a mop and a powerful vacuum to help clean up.

The firefighter can talk to ground crew via an intercom

Hand-operated nozzle

Electrically controlled nozzle

Gates on the platform open and close. Firefighters can enter or leave the platform here if necessary

Control box for the ladder

Serving Since 1889

ABERDEEN

ABERDEEN FIRE DEPT.

Pumping power

Water is pumped through two nozzles on the platform. One is electrically controlled, the other is operated by hand. Between them, they can pump about 1,500 gallons (5,600 liters) of water a minute onto a fire, attacking it from above. That's a lot of water!

Water is taken in from a water source through this hose

Air horn

These wrenches are used to tighten or loosen the hose attachments

Water is pumped onto a fire through this hose

Airport fire truck

This fire truck carries six times more water than many of the fire engines you'll see on the road. It can also pump water at least four times faster. The truck has to be able to carry and pump more water as the incidents it is called to may not always be near a water source.

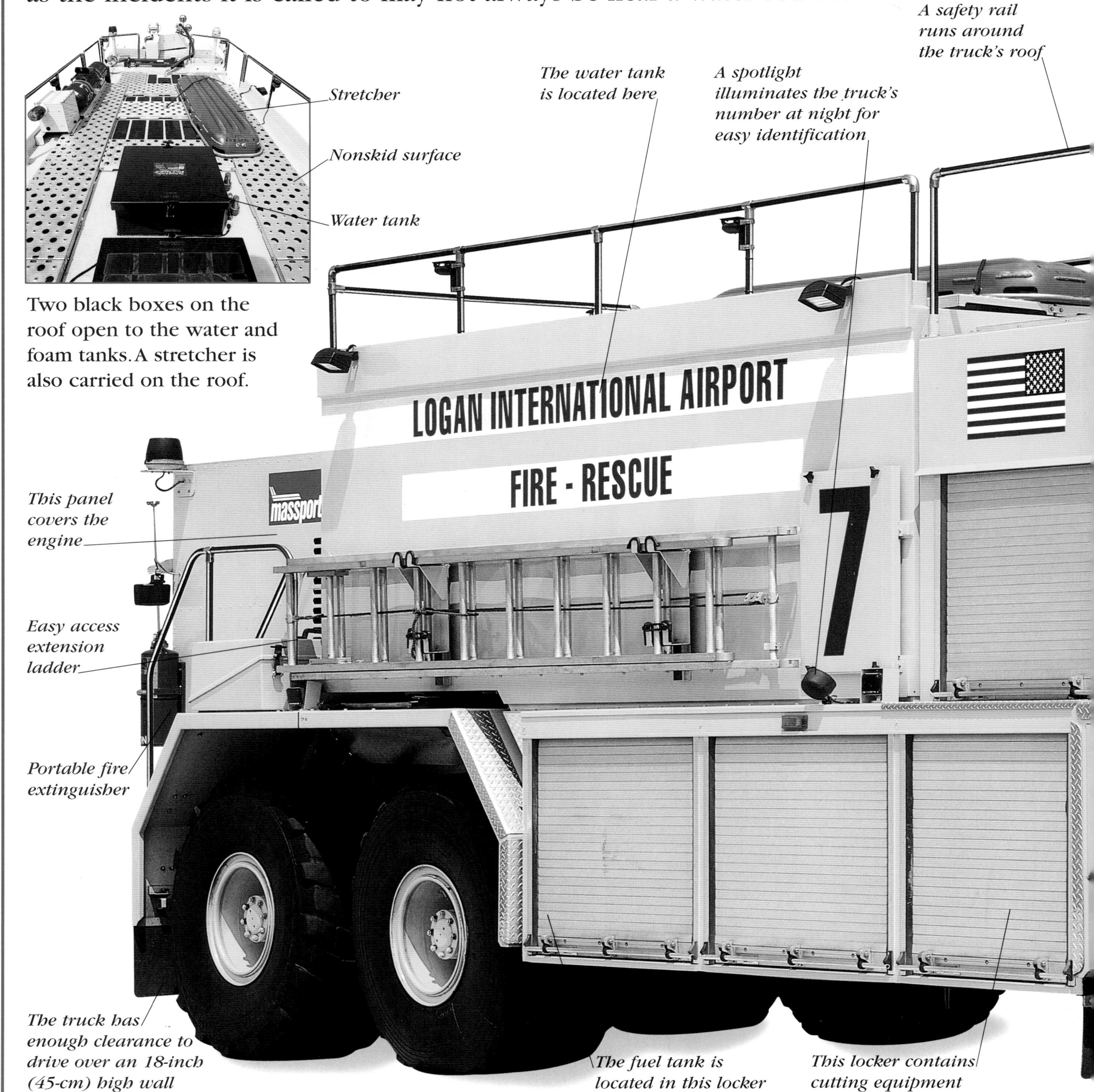

Two black boxes on the roof open to the water and foam tanks. A stretcher is also carried on the roof.

Finding and flooding a hot spot

On top of the driver's cab is a heat-seeking camera. This is linked up to a screen in the cab where the crew are able to see hot spots inside an airplane. Hot spots show up on the screen as areas of white. The firefighters can then target this area with the two nozzles at the front of the truck, controlling them with joy sticks. To fire a jet of water a firefighter simply squeezes a button.

Airport firefighters dress in a fire-retardant suit and carry an air supply.

Heavy rescue truck

Some emergencies require extra help, and this amazing fire truck can provide just that. It is packed with equipment to help rescuers tackle different problems at rescue sites. It also has a huge crane that can be used to raise and lower people and equipment to exactly where needed.

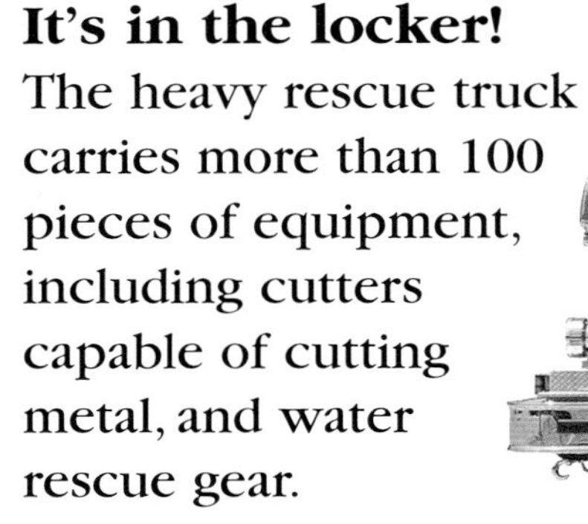

It's in the locker!
The heavy rescue truck carries more than 100 pieces of equipment, including cutters capable of cutting metal, and water rescue gear.

Crane

Harnesses

The orange sacks contain ropes

These huge cutters will open up a car in minutes

Air bottles

These air bags can be inflated to lift a heavy object

The bus-style mirrors have two parts. One gives vision close up, the other further back

Siren

The front bumper contains a winch

Two lockers in the front bumper hold chains for use with the winch

Air horn

Chocks prevent the truck from moving when the crane is in use

Winch it up

The boom extends 50 feet (15 meters) and is used to recover a car from a ditch or to stabilize a vehicle that has rolled. It is also used to lift a metal box called a trench pod off the truck and into areas where it may be required. This box contains panels and beams that are used to stabilize walls in a confined space that may otherwise collapse.

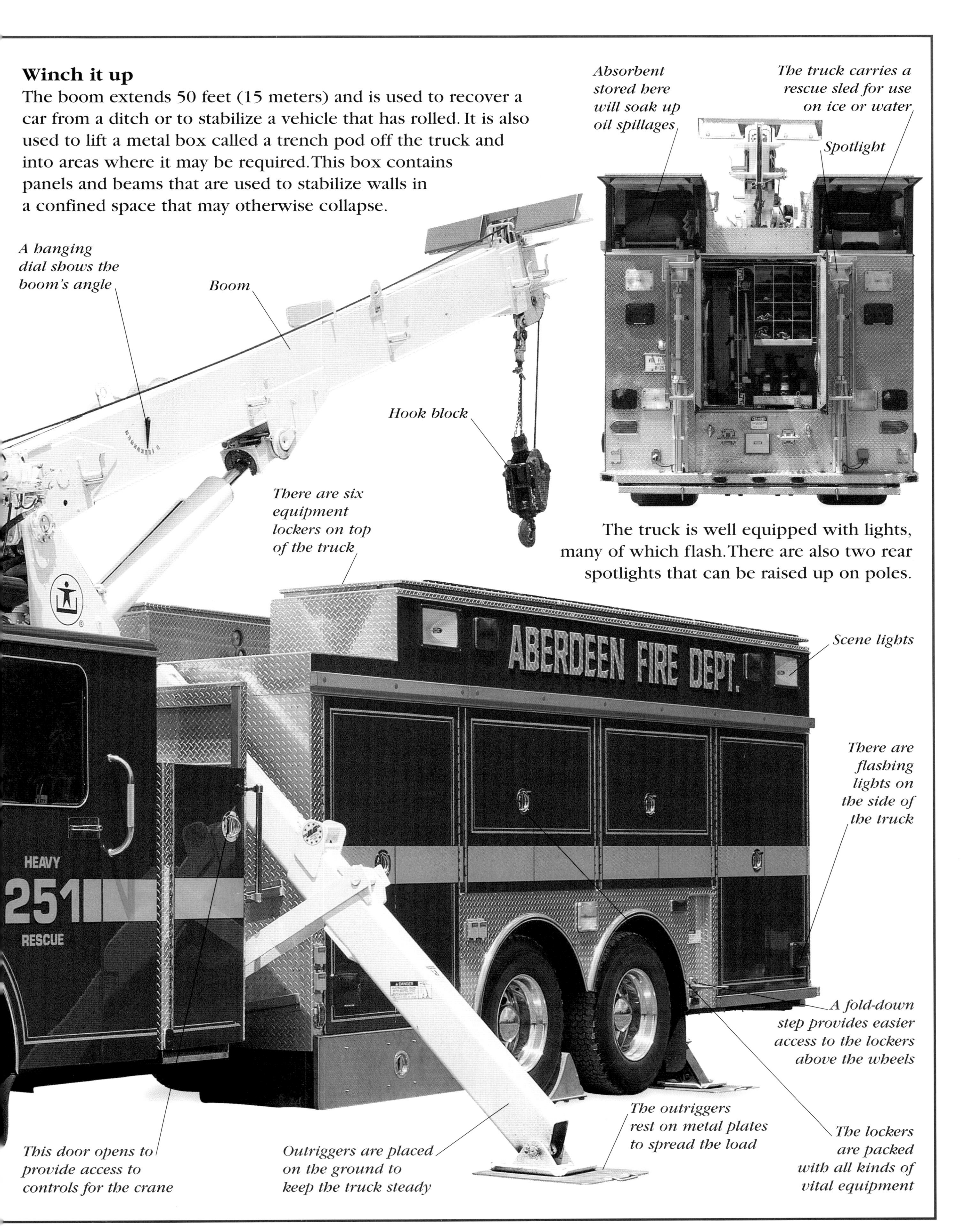

The truck is well equipped with lights, many of which flash. There are also two rear spotlights that can be raised up on poles.

Snow rescue vehicles

It can be difficult to mount a rescue operation in the snow. That's when a snowmobile can come in handy. The snowmobile's powerful motor drives a caterpillar track under the machine and propels it over the snow and ice. The driver grips handlebars attached to two metal skis at the front of the machine to carefully guide the snowmobile over the frozen landscape.

The hatch opens upward for easy access

There is no room for a first-aid kit – the casualty is taken straight to the hospital

A stretcher slides in and out through the hatch

Hidden away
The snowmobile hauls a rescue sled. Open the back of the sled and there's room inside for a casualty to ride on a stretcher. The stretcher has straps to keep the casualty immobile.

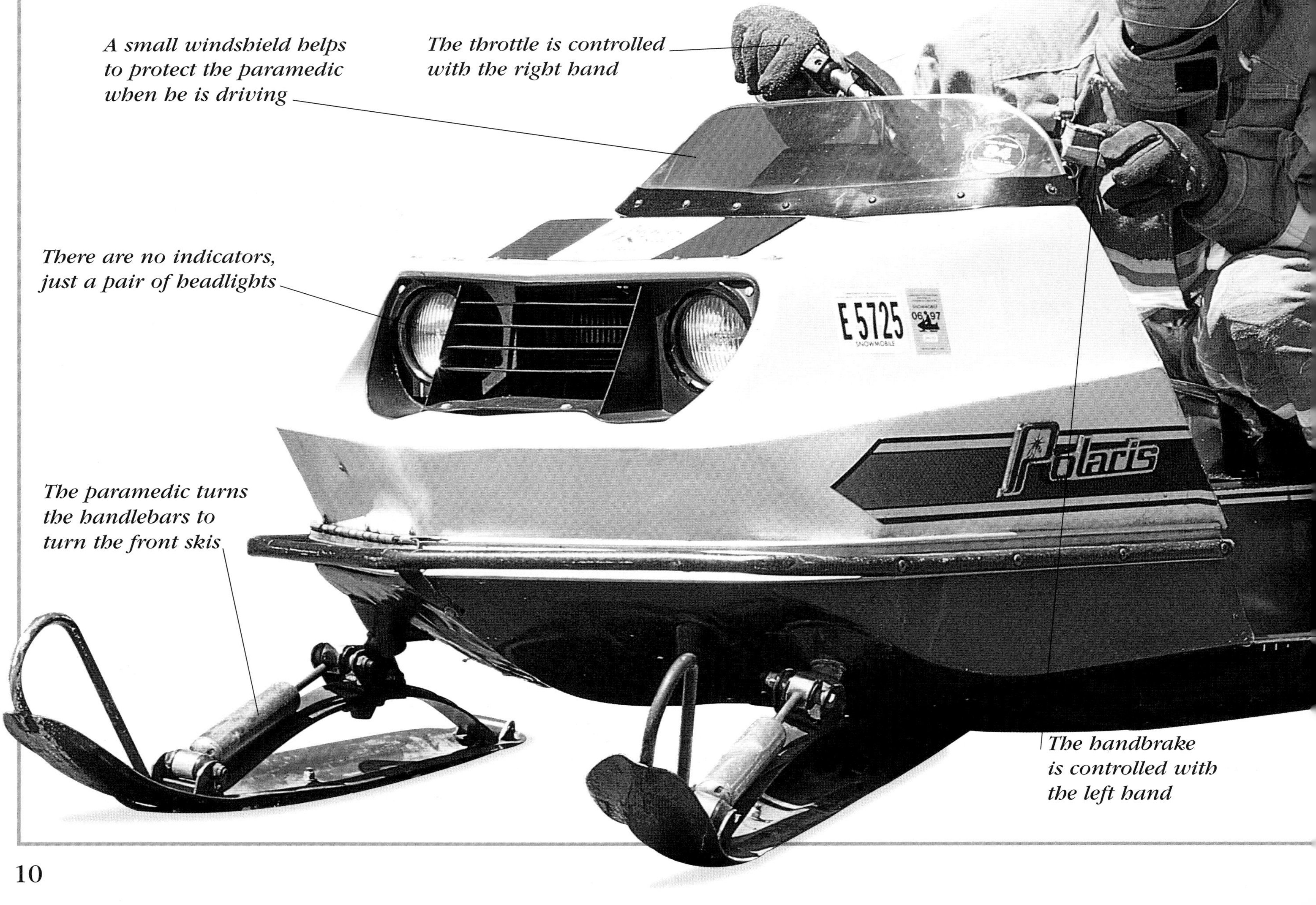

A small windshield helps to protect the paramedic when he is driving

The throttle is controlled with the right hand

There are no indicators, just a pair of headlights

The paramedic turns the handlebars to turn the front skis

The handbrake is controlled with the left hand

Fire rescue all-terrain vehicle

This unusual vehicle is used for the rescue of people and trapped animals in a mountainous area of Australia. It carries four firefighters, and plenty of rescue equipment and firefighting hoses. The rubber caterpillar tracks do less damage to the ground than tires or metal tracks. That makes it good for use in areas where ground erosion is a problem.

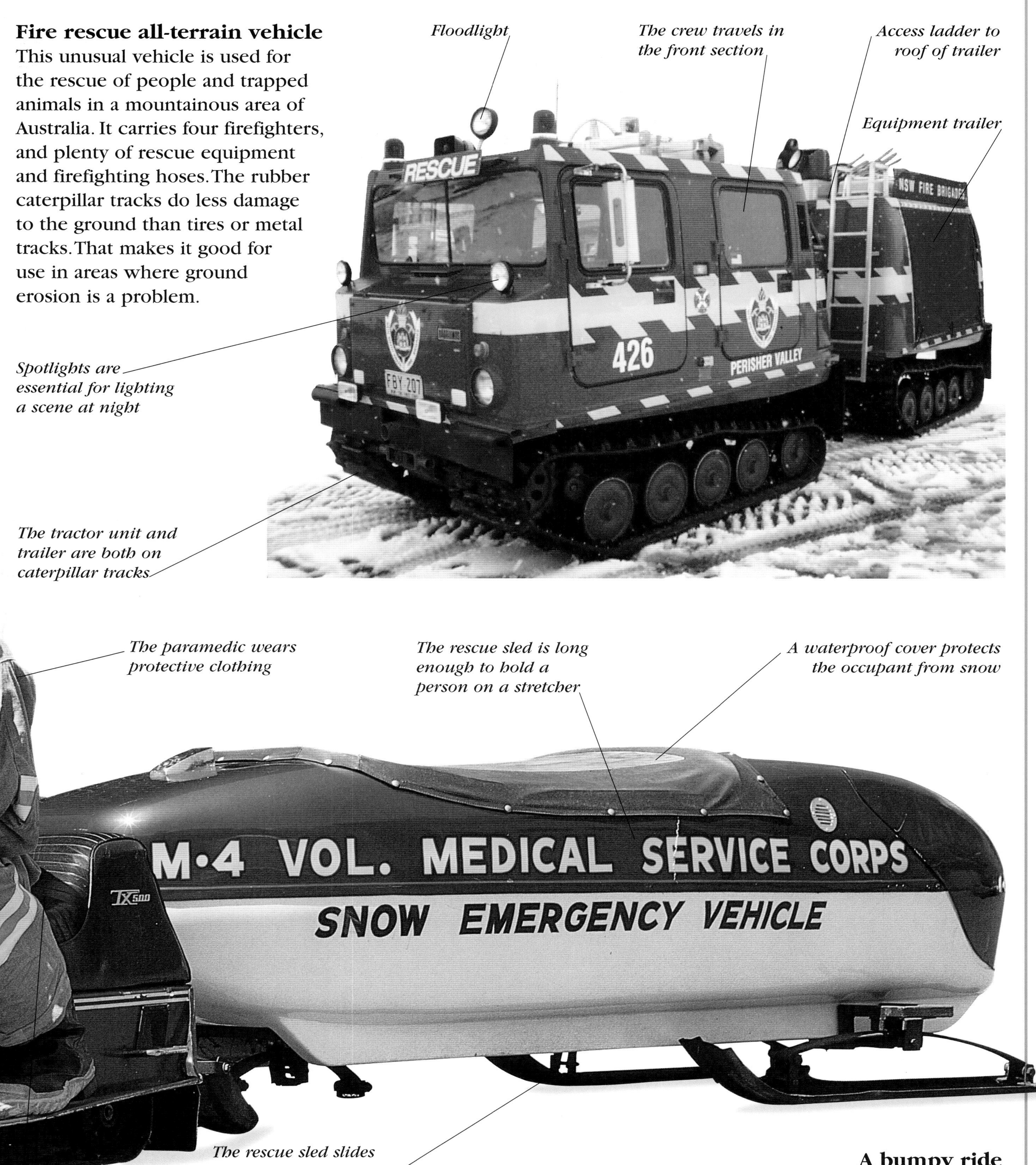

A bumpy ride

Once the paramedic has checked the casualty, he or she is strapped to the stretcher, the back is secured, and the paramedic sets off for the hospital. It can be a bumpy ride, as snow can hide debris on the path, so the paramedic will drive fairly slowly.

Ambulances

An ambulance is a welcome sight if you are injured. It is packed with first-aid equipment and carries paramedics, people who are skilled in first aid, directly to an accident. The speed with which an ambulance can weave through traffic means the paramedics will often arrive quickly enough to save a person's life. They will then work on a casualty as he or she is rushed to the hospital.

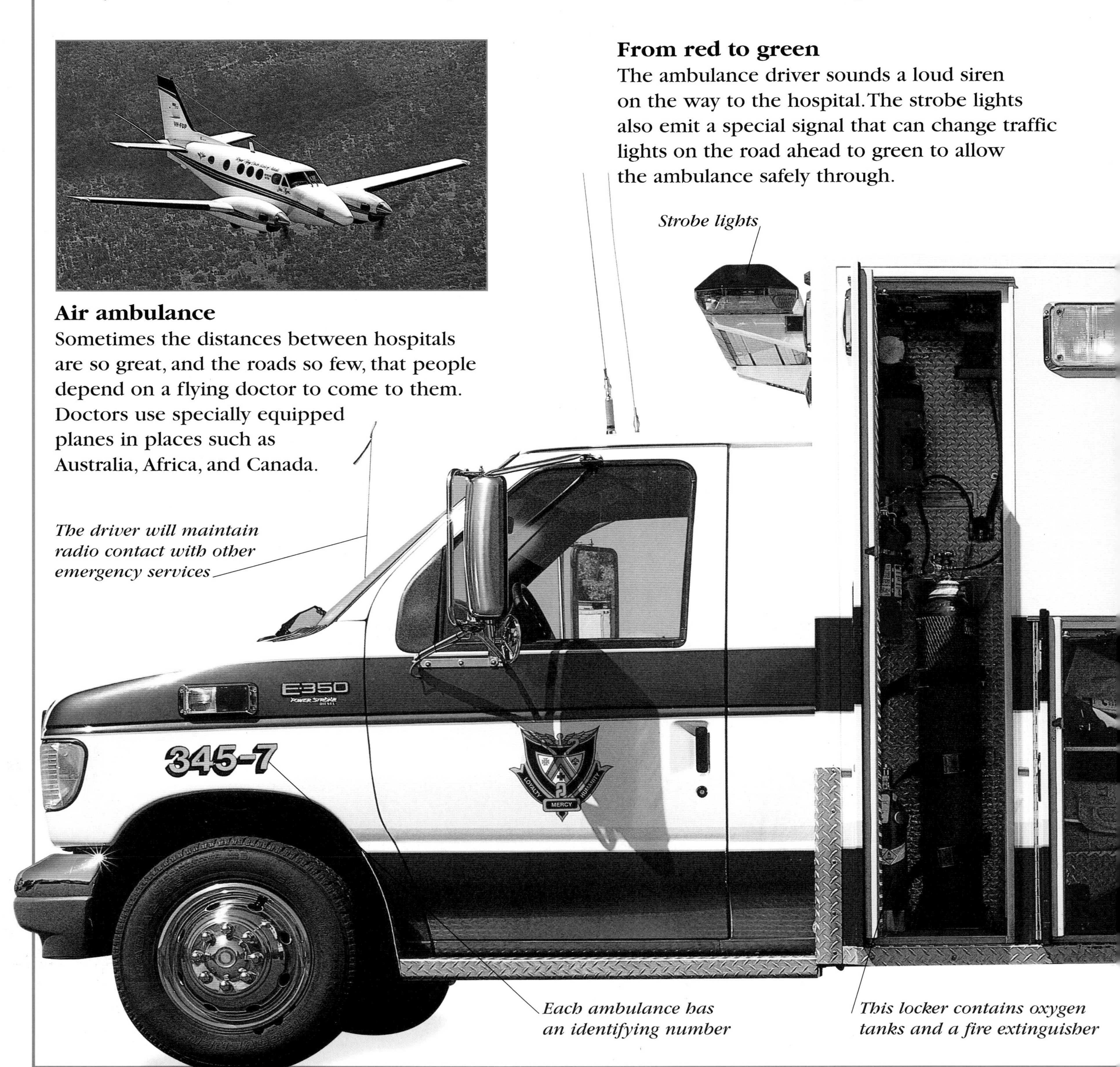

Air ambulance
Sometimes the distances between hospitals are so great, and the roads so few, that people depend on a flying doctor to come to them. Doctors use specially equipped planes in places such as Australia, Africa, and Canada.

From red to green
The ambulance driver sounds a loud siren on the way to the hospital. The strobe lights also emit a special signal that can change traffic lights on the road ahead to green to allow the ambulance safely through.

A mini-hospital

The ambulance is packed with compartments. It carries all kinds of equipment, including oxygen, blankets, stretchers, and medicines. There is even room for the paramedic to sit by the casualty as the ambulance heads for the hospital.

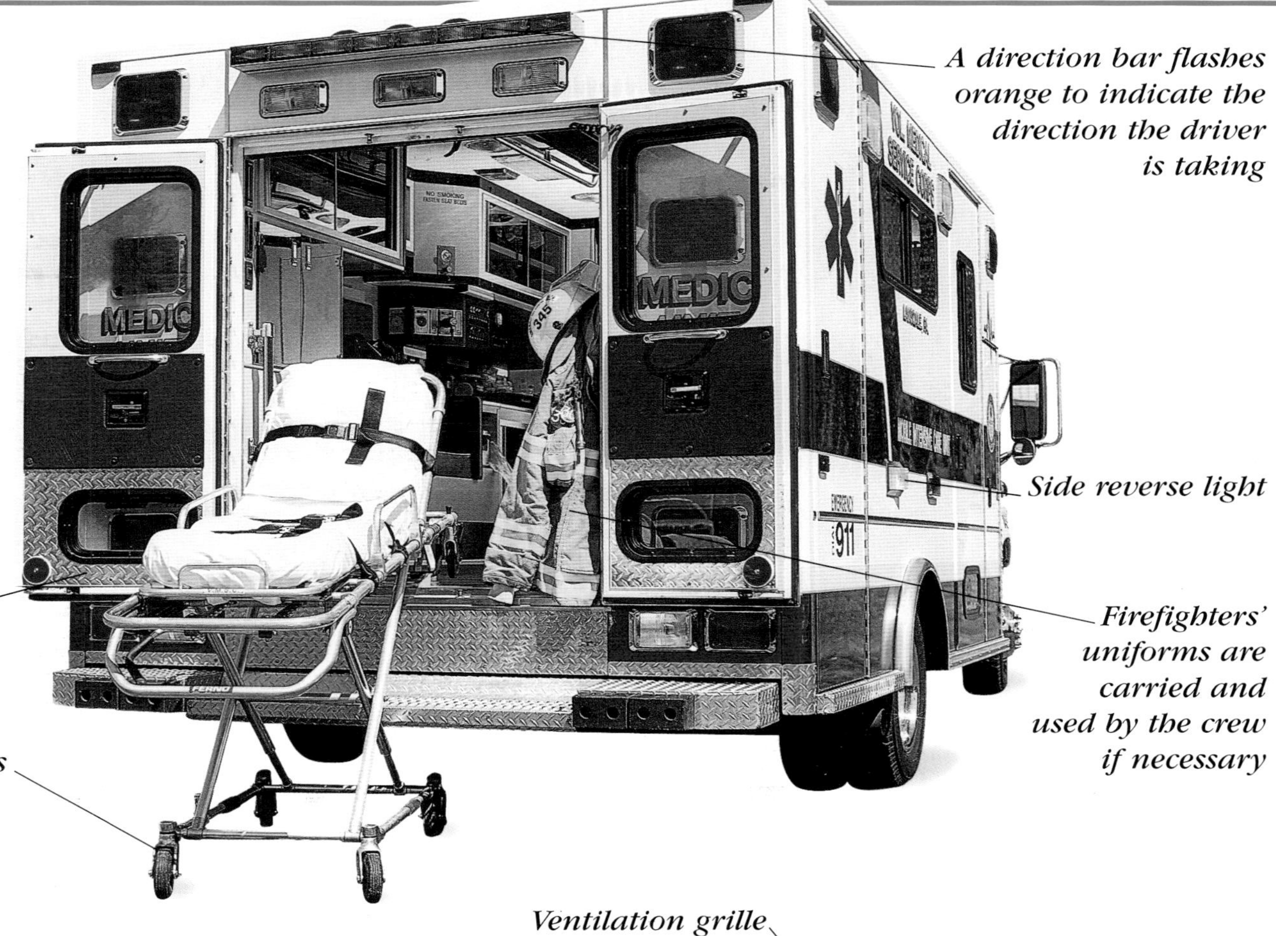

A direction bar flashes orange to indicate the direction the driver is taking

Side reverse light

Double doors provide a wide opening for the stretcher

Firefighters' uniforms are carried and used by the crew if necessary

Lightweight stretcher with scissor lift and drop wheels

The ambulance contains a small emergency room

Ventilation grille

VOL. MEDICAL
SERVICE CORPS
LANSDALE, PA.

EMERGENCY
911

The crew can also reach this locker from inside the ambulance

An equipment drawer slides out

All of the lockers have internal lights

The water is usually dropped onto the fire from a height of between 90 and 115 feet (30 and 35 meters). That's about four times the height of the airplane's tailfin.

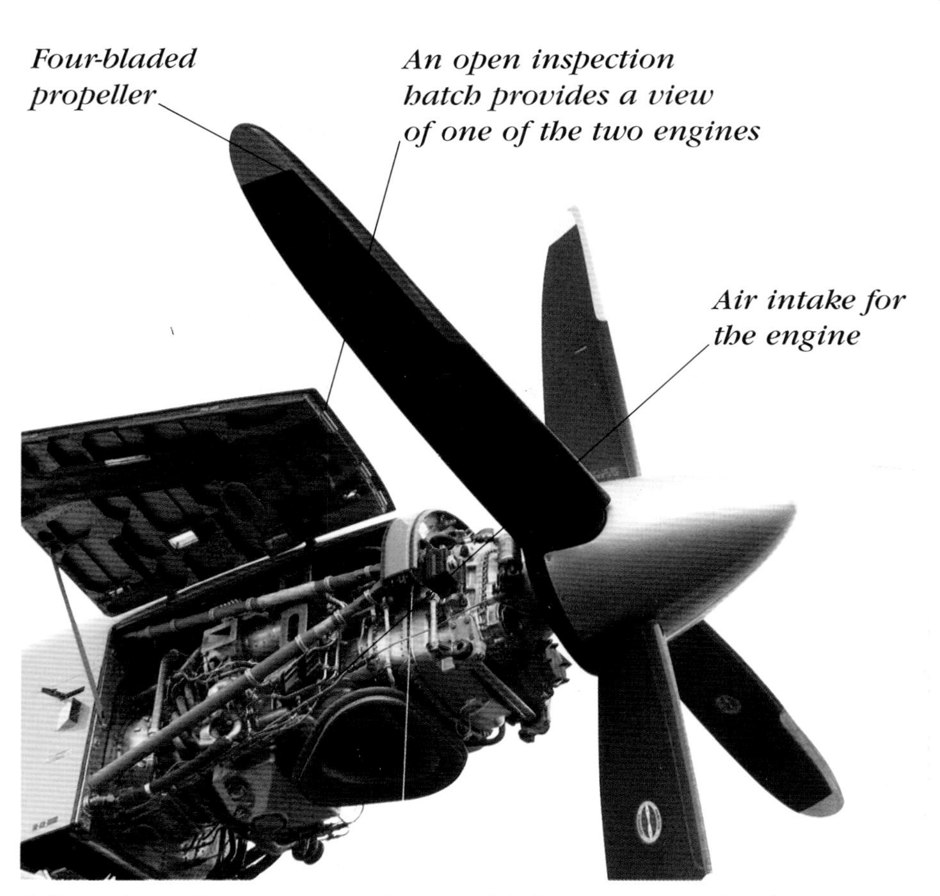

The plane has two engines which can carry it along at a top speed of 230 mph (375 kph) – or as slow as 120 mph (195 kph) when it slows down to drop its load.

The airplane's wings are unusually high to keep them clear of the water

In flight and when scooping up water, the landing gear, or wheels, are drawn up alongside the aircraft's fuselage

In flight, it is difficult to see the blades of a spinning propeller

Mountain rescue vehicle

Reaching a casualty on a hillside is tricky, especially if the weather and light are poor. This Land Rover can carry eight people toward the scene of an accident, including all the equipment they will require. Its powerful engine and high ground clearance allow it to cross deep mud and large rocks. Its engine actually provides the power of 182 horses!

The rescue team will park as close as possible to where they are required. They then unload what they need and continue on foot.

Radio antenna

Orange strips reflect light for high visibility

A metal bar helps to protect the engine

Access ladder to roof-mounted cage

Blue flashing light

Rope can be carried on top or inside

The winch has a 120-foot (36-meter) length of cable

Like all rescue vehicles, the truck has a loud siren

Equipment is stored in the back

Grilles protect the rear lights from stones

The winch is used to pull a car out of a ditch

Fire-fighting planes

When a forest fire breaks out, it's usually in a place that is hard to reach. This incredible plane can reach these places by flying in, swooping low over the flames, and dropping huge amounts of water. It can then collect more water from a lake or from the ocean to drop again and again. One of these fire-fighting airplanes has made an amazing 225 runs in a single day!

A forest fire spreads quickly, sometimes by almost 100 mph (160 kph)! A fire-fighting plane can attack it from above, often before a ground crew can reach the fire.

Swoop and scoop

The airplane collects water from a lake, river, or the ocean by swooping down and scooping it into four gigantic tanks. Then, on the way to the fire, foam is injected into the water. This mixture acts like a blanket when dropped onto a fire, helping to smother the flames.

The tailfin is just over 29 feet (9 meters) high

A wing fence improves air flow over the wing, helping to lift the plane into the air

CL-41

There are two 80-gallon (300-liter) foam reservoirs. Small amounts of foam are mixed into the water before it is dropped onto a fire

Unlike a passenger plane, there are very few windows

Anti-collision light

Tail plane

The hinged rudder is moved to turn the tail left or right

A float provides stability for water landings

Red skies!

This mighty fire-fighting plane is known as an airtanker. It carries a red liquid, called a retardant, which is dropped to create a fire line – a break between a fire and the surrounding area. The fire line gives ground crews valuable time to mount an attack on the fire. The red coloring is a vivid marker to help pilots see where they have been working, but it soon fades.

The red liquid contains fertilizer, gum arabic, red iron oxide, and water to slow and cool the fire. The fertilizer helps new growth.

All airtankers have a different number or call sign

Cockpit

This airtanker has four engines

The doors to the tanks are computer controlled

Wing flaps

The retardant is carried in massive 3,000-gallon (11,000-liter) tanks in the plane's belly

All packed up

A sturdy roof cage holds equipment too large to be easily stowed away inside the vehicle. On the top are two fold-up stretchers. Equipment packed away inside includes lighting, an extensive first-aid kit, more than 2,000 feet (600 meters) of rope, snow chains, axes, a sleeping bag, and a tent.

This antenna allows contact with helicopter crews

There is an information board behind the passengers' seats

Flashing light bar

Steps fold down for easier access

Mudguard

Lockers beneath the seats store additional equipment, including flares, binoculars, and a tow rope

All-terrain tires for offroad use

The four-compartment, four-door water tank system is located in the belly of the plane's fuselage. The tankshold 1,620 gallons (6,130 liters) – 12 loads from this plane could fill a swimming pool!

Hidden dangers

The pilot has a dangerous job. The ride will be bumpy due to turbulence in the air from the fire. He or she might have to scoop from restricted spaces, and maneuver the aircraft at low speeds and low altitude. The plane is checked after each mission.

When the propellers spin, they force air back, pushing the plane forward

Cockpit

The body or fuselage is shaped like a ship's hull

Retractable nose landing gear

Access door to cockpit

The pilot can complete each scoop in less than 12 seconds

Wing endplates make the airplane easier to fly

Large cockpit windows allow the pilot a good view of the fire below

The wingspan is just over 93 feet (28 meters)

The plane's distinctive yellow coloring is an instantly recognizable and welcome sight

The plane can scoop from water as shallow as 6 feet (2 meters)

The water bomber can land on and take off from water – even if there are waves that are 4 feet (1.2 meters) high

Fire-fighting helicopter

The pilot can vary the flow of water dropped, from a light mist to a heavy torrent. In fact, the whole tankful can be dropped in three seconds.

Fire-fighting planes are not the only machines that can attack a fire from the air. Helicopters have been developed to do the same task. However, unlike a plane, a helicopter can hover in the same place to make a precise water drop. This helicopter can also pick up water from a pond so shallow that you could stand in it!

A hidden help

The pilot can make use of the downwash, or wind created by the helicopter's rotors, to push smoke aside temporarily. This can help the pilot to spot the heart of a fire, allowing him or her to identify the best way to attack the blaze.

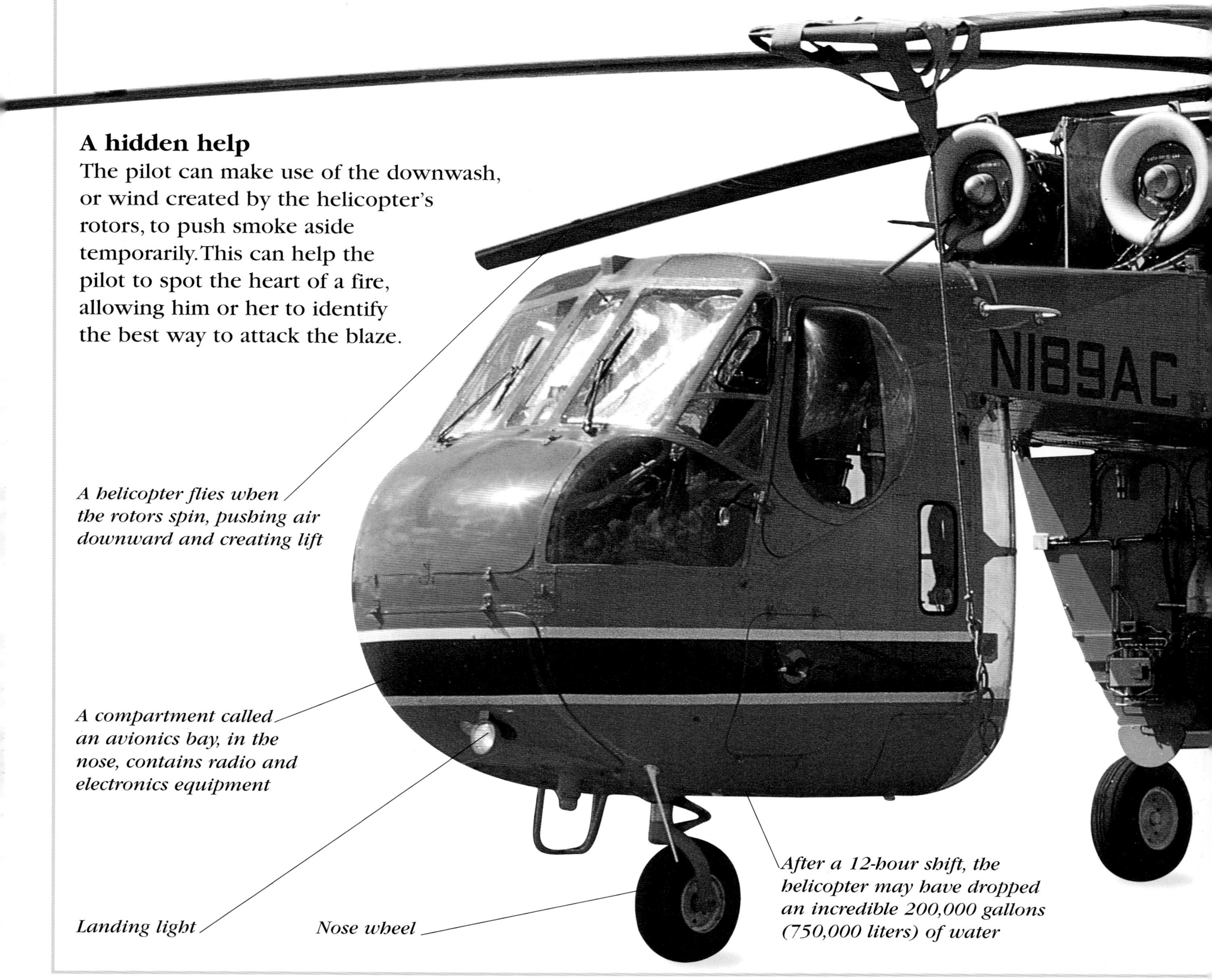

A helicopter flies when the rotors spin, pushing air downward and creating lift

A compartment called an avionics bay, in the nose, contains radio and electronics equipment

Landing light

Nose wheel

After a 12-hour shift, the helicopter may have dropped an incredible 200,000 gallons (750,000 liters) of water

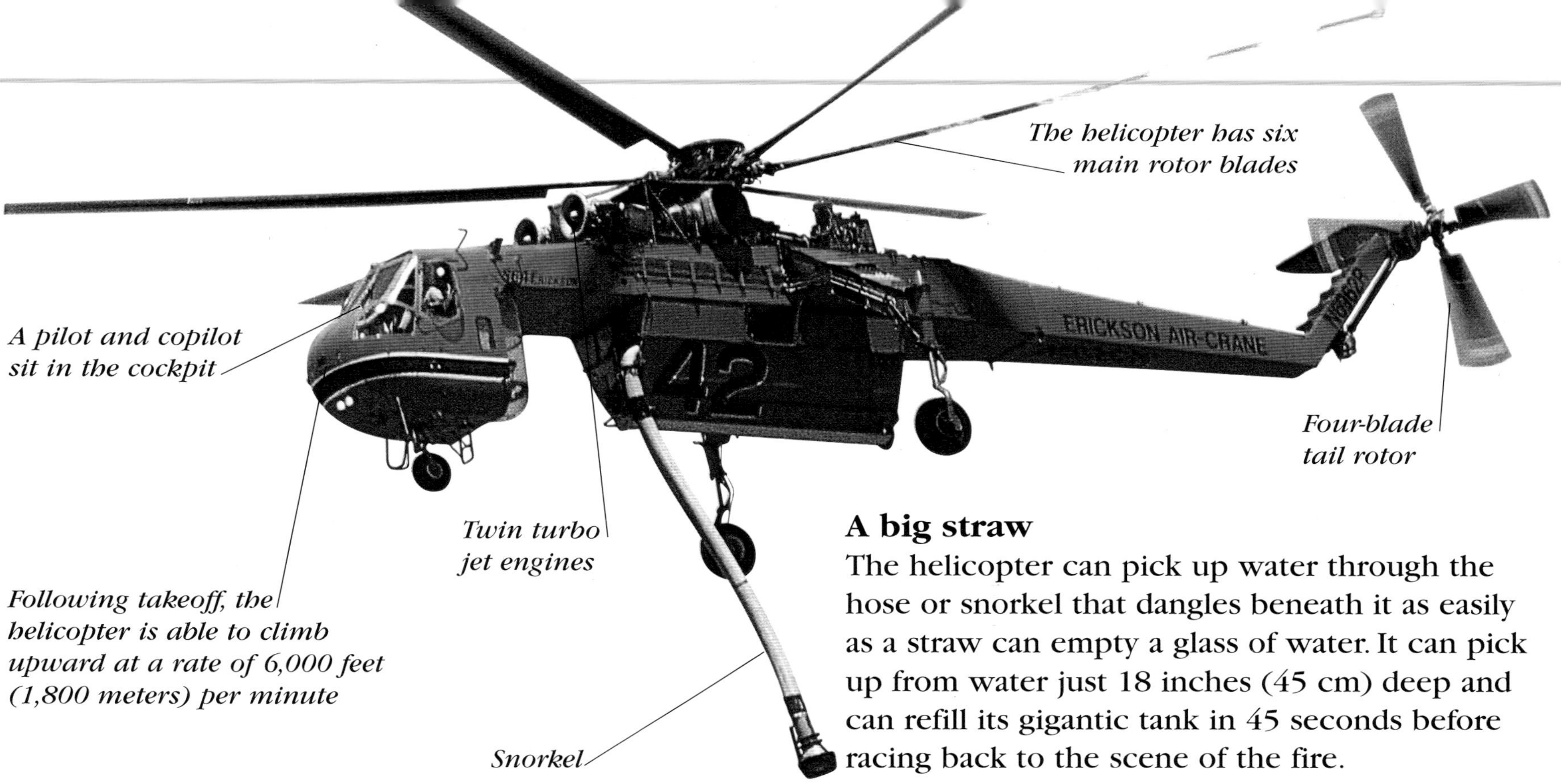
The helicopter has six main rotor blades
A pilot and copilot sit in the cockpit
Four-blade tail rotor
Twin turbo jet engines
Following takeoff, the helicopter is able to climb upward at a rate of 6,000 feet (1,800 meters) per minute
Snorkel
ERICKSON AIR-CRANE
42

A big straw

The helicopter can pick up water through the hose or snorkel that dangles beneath it as easily as a straw can empty a glass of water. It can pick up from water just 18 inches (45 cm) deep and can refill its gigantic tank in 45 seconds before racing back to the scene of the fire.

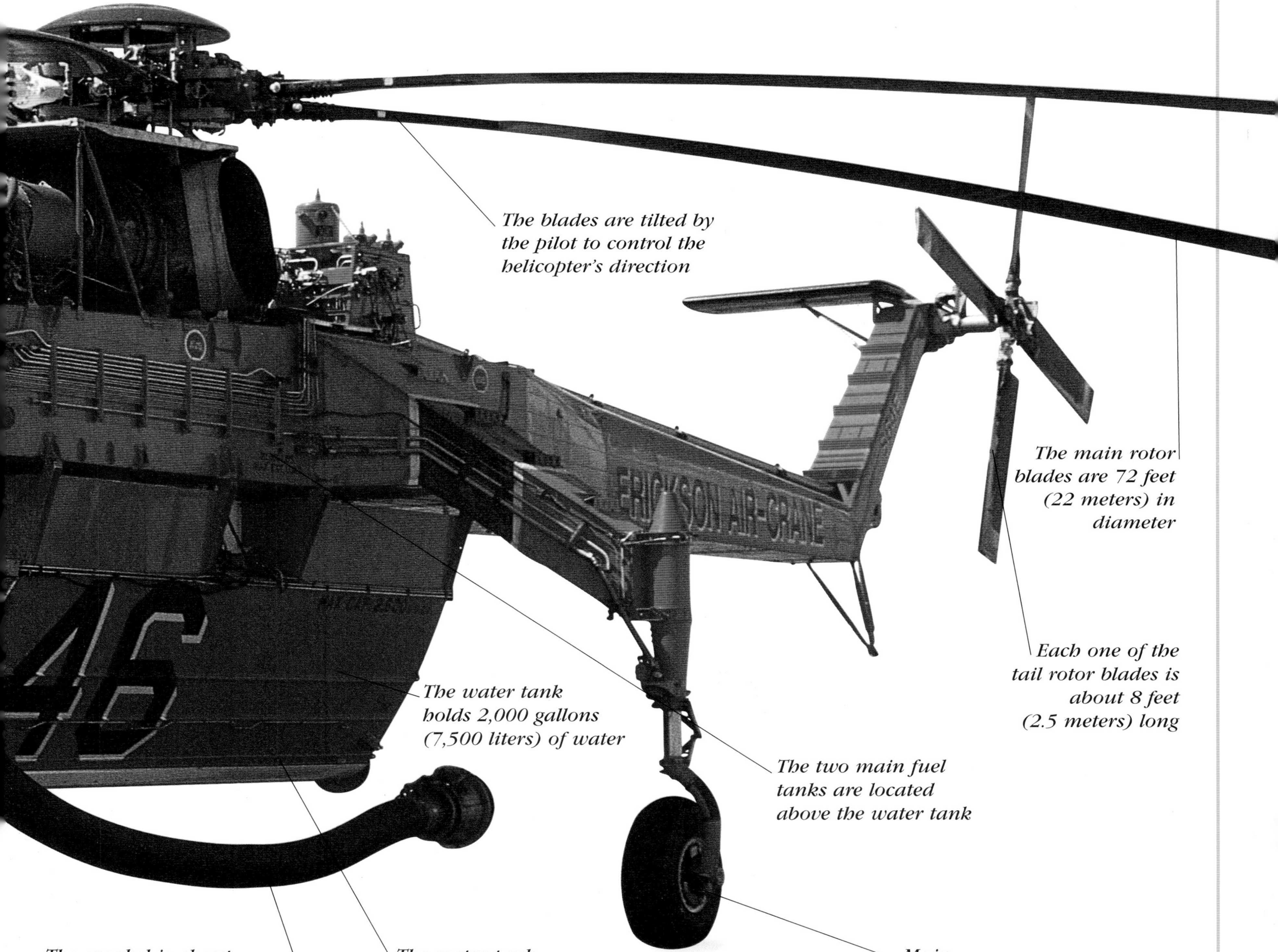
The blades are tilted by the pilot to control the helicopter's direction
The main rotor blades are 72 feet (22 meters) in diameter
Each one of the tail rotor blades is about 8 feet (2.5 meters) long
The water tank holds 2,000 gallons (7,500 liters) of water
The two main fuel tanks are located above the water tank
The snorkel is about 26 feet (8 meters) in length
The water tank has double doors
Main landing gear
ERICKSON AIR-CRANE
46

Rescue helicopter

A helicopter is ideal for rescuing people from a mountain, from the sea, or for collecting a casualty from a boat. It will hover above the spot where it is needed, and lower a winchman and medical bag. If necessary, the winchman can descend 245 feet (75 meters) on a steel cable, though most winch drops are shorter. The winchman then brings the casualty back up to the helicopter, by stretcher if necessary.

Each of the five rotor blades is about 30 feet (9 meters) in length

In flight, the pilot changes the angle of the rotor blades to control direction

A dome covers the radar scanner

The helicopter's rotor blades can be folded if it is carried on a ship

Helping the search

This helicopter is called a Sea King. It is well-equipped for search and rescue, with navigational aids which enable it to pinpoint a distress signal from a long way away. Night vision equipment also allows the crew to see distress flares from a greater distance than they might otherwise.

An anti-collision light flashes white. It is switched to red as the helicopter approaches a rescue

Winch

UHF aerial

The small tail rotor blades stop the helicopter from spinning around

The helicopter's tail can be folded to the side when it is carried on a ship

Sliding winch door

The helicopter can carry 17 people, including its crew of four. It carries two stretchers.

Though it looks like a grab rail, this is actually an antenna

Flotation bags inflate if the helicopter has to make an emergency landing on water

The winch is worked by the winch operator, who uses a control panel just inside the open winch door.

All-weather lifeboat

The emergency call or "shout" comes in and the six-person crew of the all-weather lifeboat drop whatever they are doing and rush to board the boat. They cast off and are then briefed on who is in trouble at sea. The lifeboat will head out in stormy seas, and can carry up to 78 survivors back to shore!

There are two steering positions. One is in the main cabin and the other is outside on the top deck.

Power pack

The lifeboat is equipped with two engines, each the length of a small car. They are the same as the engines used to drive large, earth-moving trucks; in fact, the combined power would equal that of more than 1,000 horses! Together, the engines gulp about 50 gallons (230 liters) of diesel fuel per hour.

A small inflatable rescue boat is carried on the top deck

This "A-frame" is used to hoist people out of the water

Each of the two life buoys is equipped with lights that float

Emergency inflatable life raft

The stern is the back of a boat

RNLB THE DUKE

Lifeboats

Royal National Lifeboat Institution

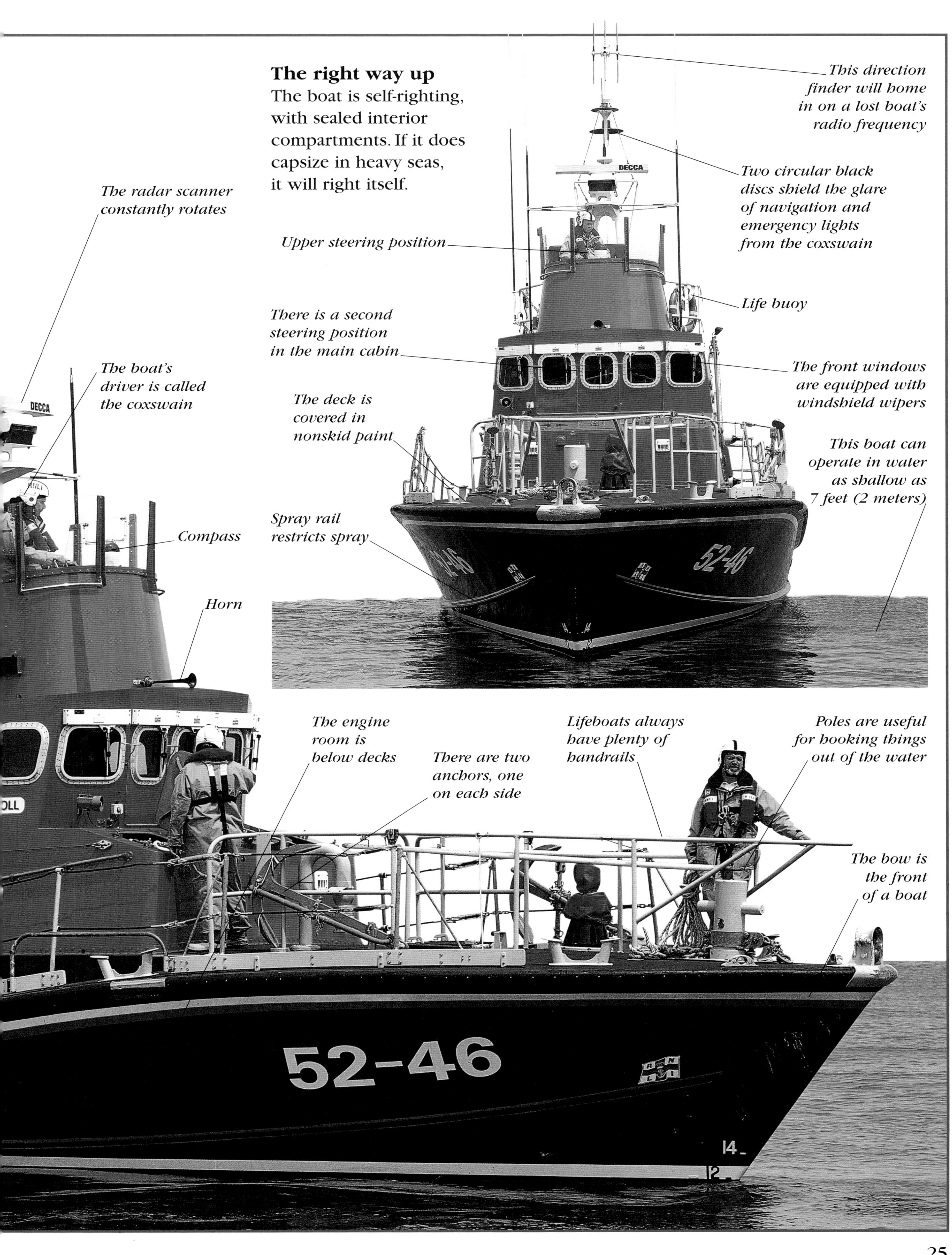

The right way up
The boat is self-righting, with sealed interior compartments. If it does capsize in heavy seas, it will right itself.

Inshore lifeboat

An inshore lifeboat is ideal for rescuing people in trouble close to shore. It might race to find a jet ski that has broken down or pick up a child whose dinghy has drifted too far out. It is faster than a larger lifeboat, and its fuel tanks can keep it going at top speed for three hours.

All sealed up

The inshore lifeboat has a shaped plastic hull. An inflatable tube, called a sponson, runs around the top of the hull. Both the hull and the sponson are divided into watertight compartments, so if one section is damaged, the boat will still float. It is known as a rigid inflatable boat, or RIB.

The two outboard motors are waterproofed. If the boat capsizes, they will restart!

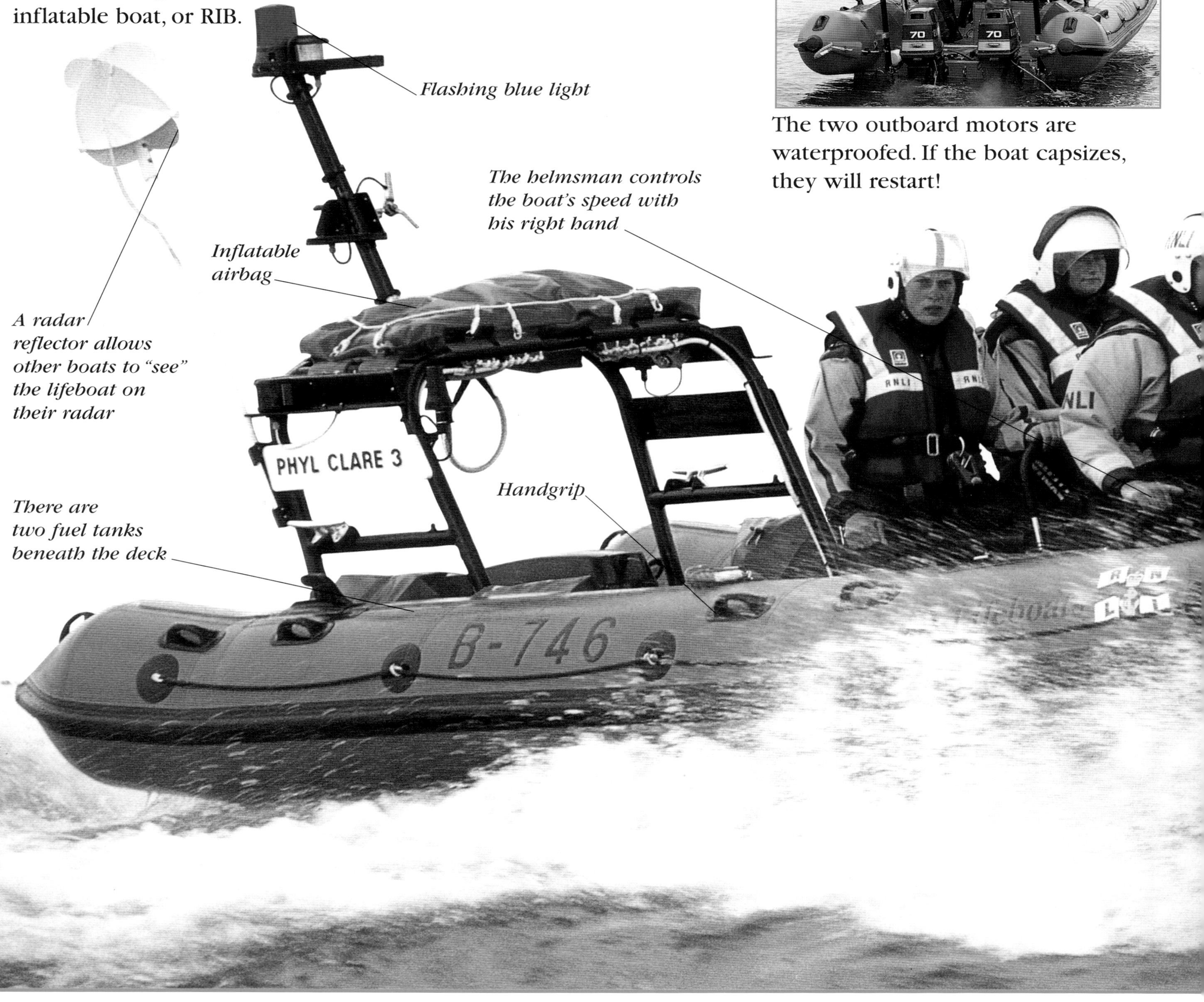

Radio antenna

Flashing blue light

The helmsman controls the boat's speed with his right hand

Inflatable airbag

A radar reflector allows other boats to "see" the lifeboat on their radar

Handgrip

There are two fuel tanks beneath the deck

PHYL CLARE 3

B-746

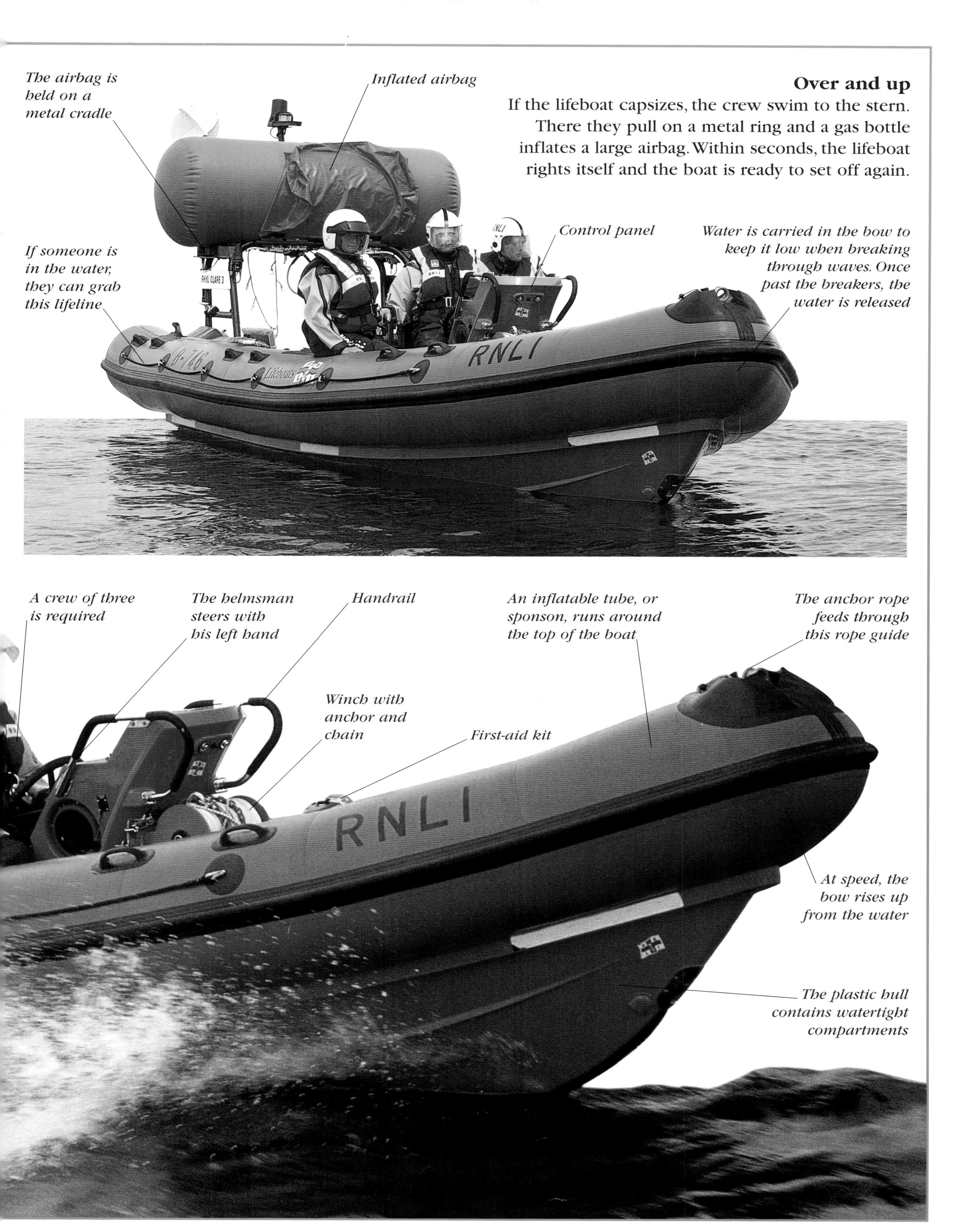

Over and up

If the lifeboat capsizes, the crew swim to the stern. There they pull on a metal ring and a gas bottle inflates a large airbag. Within seconds, the lifeboat rights itself and the boat is ready to set off again.

Rescue hovercraft

If somebody needs help, but their boat is stuck on a shoal, a hovercraft is the only land-based vehicle that can easily reach them. This hovercraft can also negotiate high seas and strong winds to search for a boat in trouble. It is an incredible machine, happily passing over a variety of ground surfaces yet leaving less of an impression on sand than a footprint!

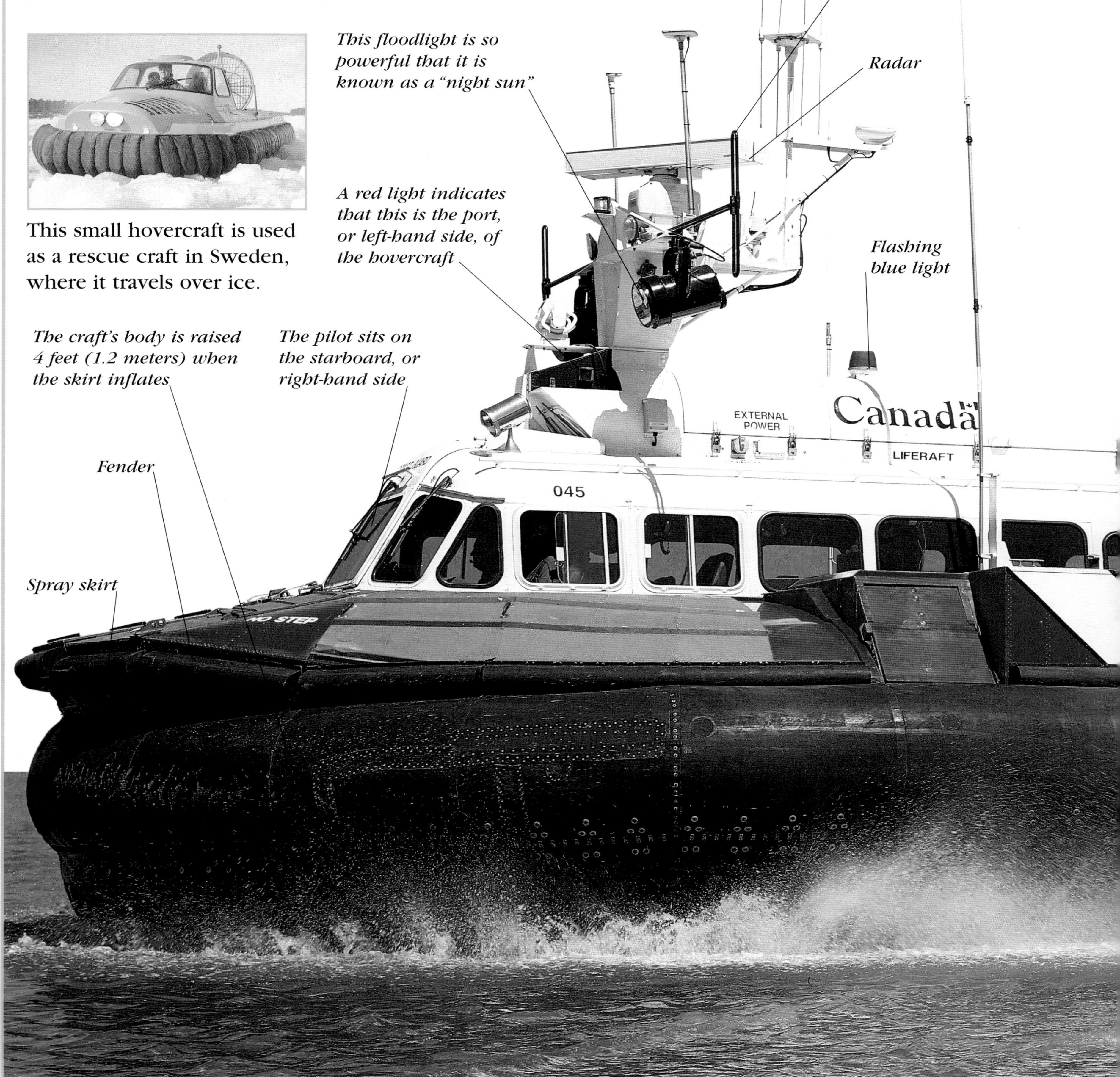

This small hovercraft is used as a rescue craft in Sweden, where it travels over ice.

Ready and waiting

Between rescue calls, the hovercraft is left open and ready to go. It is always refueled and its batteries recharged when it comes in. The crew of four can respond to a call and be on their way within seconds.

A six-person life raft is stowed in this locker

A yellow light identifies the craft at night as a hovercraft

Three-bladed propeller

An anchor and line is kept in here in case of breakdown

Bow ramp

The hovercraft can travel onto land to pass a patient directly over to an ambulance crew

Emergency exit window

Floating on air

A hovercraft travels on a cushion of air, which is sucked in through a huge lift fan to fill the skirt. The skirt is made of strips of rubber fingers covered by a spray skirt. Altogether the craft is very fast and highly maneuverable.

A gigantic lift fan 7 feet (2 meters) across is located under the exhaust pipe

Rudders are used for changes of direction

The engine is located here

Exhaust pipe

The hovercraft is able to tow a boat from its stern if necessary

Fireboat

Fires occasionally break out in buildings right next to harbors, or on boats. A fireboat can flood these fires within seconds as water is pumped directly from the endless supply surrounding the boat.

The fireboat can pump about 7,500 gallons (34,000 liters) of water a minute. That's five times more than a large fire engine you'll see on the street.

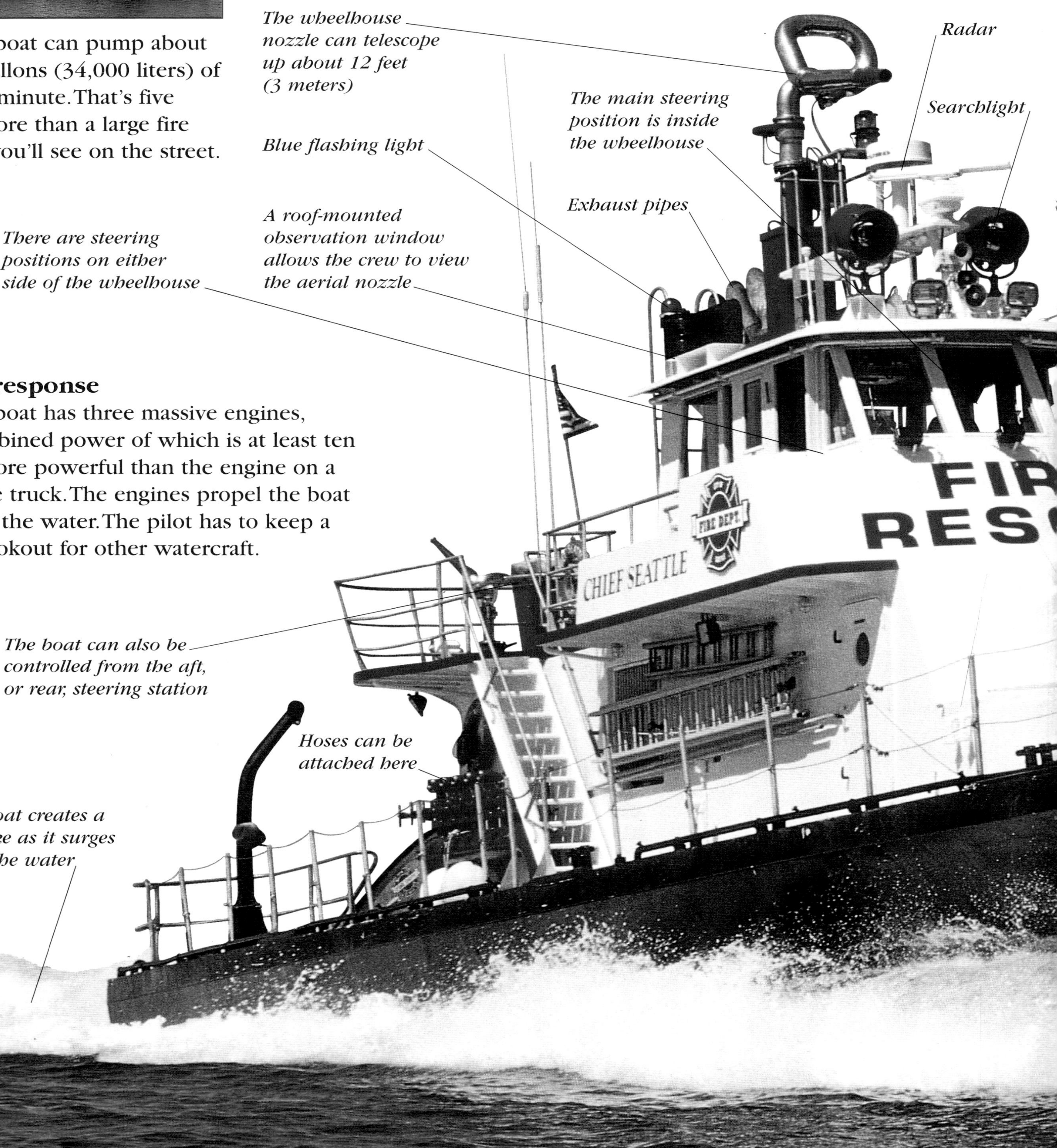

Rapid response

The fireboat has three massive engines, the combined power of which is at least ten times more powerful than the engine on a large fire truck. The engines propel the boat through the water. The pilot has to keep a sharp lookout for other watercraft.

The fireboat carries many of the things an ordinary fire engine would carry, including fire suits and boots, protective helmets, shovels, hoses, a chain saw, and ladders.

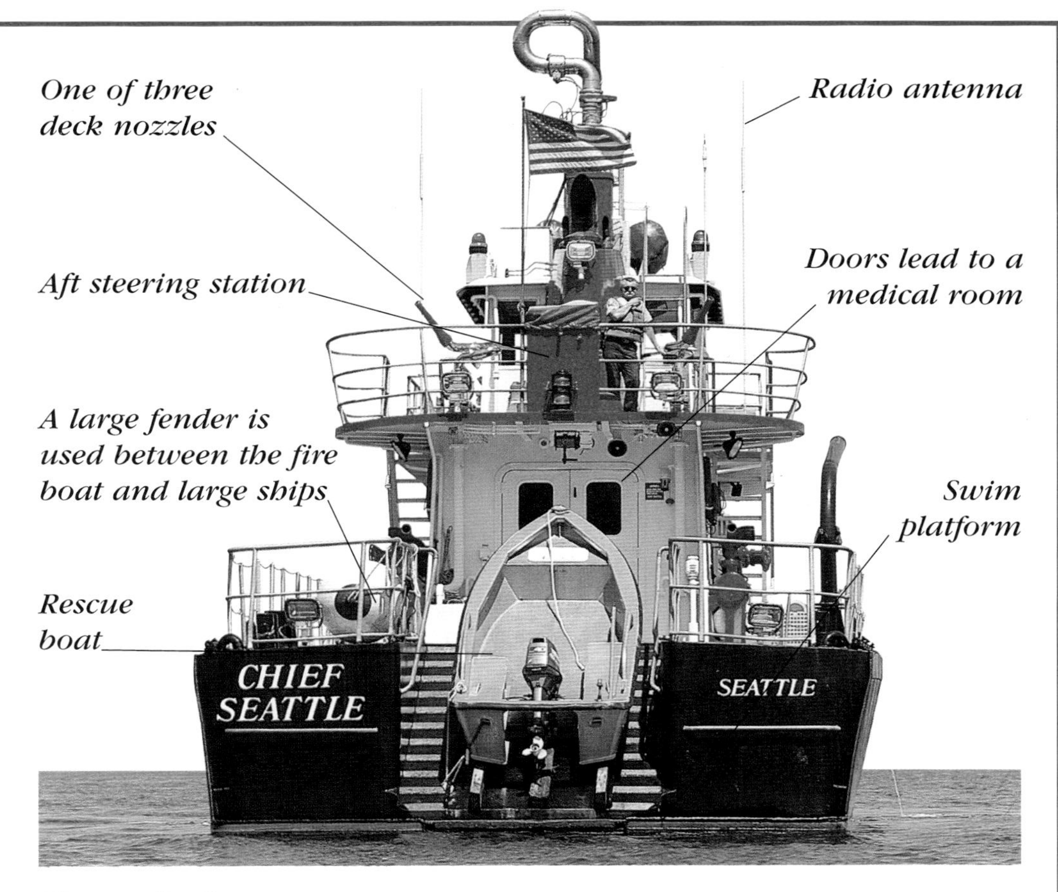

Extra help

A small rescue/under pier boat is carried at the stern of the boat. It may be used to take a hose under a pier or bridge or to rescue people from the water. It is winched down a ramp and passes over a swim platform to reach the water.

Port steering position

Siren

The boat carries foam tanks. Foam is mixed with water to fight oil-based fires

Foredeck nozzle

A nozzle is set into the hull on each side of the boat

There is a kitchen and toilet area below the foredeck

Bow

Although large, the boat can operate in just 7 feet (2 meters) of water

Water is pumped in through the base of the hull to feed the nozzles

CHIEF SEATTLE

Glossary

Absorbent
A material which a fire crew use to soak up oil spills.

Aft
The area toward the back of a boat or aircraft.

Airbag
A bag which can be inflated with air and used for buoyancy or for lifting heavy objects.

Avionics
An aircraft's electronic and navigation equipment.

Bow
The front of a boat

Cockpit
The cabin at the front of an aircraft which houses the controls used to make it fly. The pilot sits in the cockpit.

Coxswain
The captain of a lifeboat.

Foredeck
The deck toward the front of a boat.

Fuselage
The body of an aircraft.

Helmsman
The captain of a small boat.

Indicators
Lights which flash orange to tell drivers whether a vehicle is turning left or right.

Outrigger
An extending leg which stabilizes a road machine.

Port
The left-hand side of a ship or aircraft.

Propeller
The blades that rotate to push a boat or aircraft through water or through air.

Radar
A navigation system which uses radio waves to locate objects. Some rescue vehicles depend on radar for finding people who need help.

Rotor blades
The long arms that rotate to lift a helicopter.

Rudder
A flap on an aircraft or boat that turns to turn the craft left or right.

Siren
The device used to make a noise to alert people that a rescue machine is in a hurry.

Sponson
Sponsons help to stabilize a boat or amphibious aircraft on the water. They are filled with air.

Starboard
The right-hand side of a ship or aircraft.

Stern
The back of a boat.

UHF
A radio frequency. The letters stand for Ultra High Frequency.

Wheelhouse
The cabin on a boat which houses the controls.

Index